Cumbrian Lines

Also by Che Chidi Chukwumerije:

<u>Prose</u>
Twice is not enough
The Lake of Love
There Is Always Something More (short stories / thoughts)

<u>Poetry</u>
Palm Lines
River
The Beautiful Ones Have Been Born
Writing Is The Happiness of Sorrow
Light of Awakening

Der Schlaf, aus dem ich wachend träume (german)
Das dauerhafte Gedicht (german)
Innengart (german)

Mmiri a zoro nwayọ nwayọ (igbo)

<u>For children</u>
Somayinozo's Stories

Che Chidi Chukwumerije
Cumbrian Lines: Poems born of the Lake District.
Second edition 2015.
First e-edition appeared 2013 under the psedonym Aka Teraka
First published as paperback in 2011.
Boxwood Publishing House e.K.
Copyright © Che Chidi Chukwumerije 2011.
All rights reserved.
ISBN 978-3-943000-58-0
Cover photo © Yvonne Chukwumerije.

CHE CHIDI CHUKWUMERIJE

CUMBRIAN LINES

Poems born of the Lake District

...

Boxwood Publishing House, Frankfurt.

Table of Contents

Part I: *The spirit of places*

Part II: *Intuitions*

Part III: *To leave is to stay*

Epilogue

for Yvonne,
with whom I walked
these hills...

1.

THE SPIRIT OF PLACES

BOATRIDE ON ULLSWATER

A life I've lived before?
Or just a summer lore?
These Cumbrian hills that float past me
Fade away, misty, like a memory

If greens could speak of all they hold
Unbroken sap, unspoken, old
Unwoken, untapped, a silent audience
Events absorbed in quiet clairaudience

What tales untold of eras lost
Would now unfold, unthawed of frost
Unbound by dust; behold, forever green
The mist has parted as though it had never been

Ullswater, whose water first watered your past
Whose feet were those that were the last
To tread that dry ground that is now your wet floor
Before that time vanished foreverevermore?

The boatride, like a gentle slide, into a strange intuition
A short sad season of startling fruition
Goodbye again, Watervalley, deep within your heart
Remember still my footsteps, there they did start

Mist and misty, mistier than thought
Misty mysteries yet they are not.
A heart is a storehouse of long forgotten memories
That sometimes arise cloaked as imagined stories

What do I have more precious than my heart,
My past's library, my future's chart.
Silently we walk, simple human beings
Yet mightier each than the sum of all worldly things.

HAWKSHEAD

If Heart could speak on its own
Without Brain as translator
Spoke its Intuition alone
Unmindful of intellect, that imitator
What startling things, yet unknown
Would fill the world's books?
What silent waters, from their deep zone
Would rise as bubbling brooks?

If there were Child in Adult
Awake, seeing, hearing, speaking
If adults would spare themselves the insult
Of hiding the child they in themselves are keeping

How different every day would feel
Refreshing, natural
With the adult balancing the child's zeal
And the child making the adult more natural...

Youth, so important
Magic Time between two times
Child and adult merge concordant
Complementing each other like natural rhymes –
What you are in your youth is what you'll be forever
Deep within your heart –
The heart speaks its mind but once, and never
Again from that path will depart.

ATOP CASTLERIGG

It must have been on Castlerigg
Amidst the ancient stones
My spirit suddenly grew big –
Did I sense my old bones?
I felt that here within this circle
I have married you before
What some might call insensible
Or, being kind, a lore…

Why do I feel what I feel?
Your eyes tell me it's real…
If you agree with me, then nothing else matters
Sacred are family matters –

I still see Castlerigg
The heart of a mighty circle
Of mountainous hills wise and big
Like a prototype stone circle
Built by Substantiate Beings
That walked the earth
Long before Human Beings
First came to birth.

Cumbrian Lines

A BEND IN THE ROAD BETWEEN GRASMERE AND RYDAL

My heart won't stop beating
The urge to remember
A certain curve of the road
That leads out of Grasmere
Towards Rydal
Where the motor road and the lake
Part the wanderer's feet
Step upon an earthen path that shall
Unhurrying though the trees
Curve the curving lake into the little bridge
At the lake's dove tail, brought us
To the shore at the foot of a hill
Where, turning, we face
Far across Grasmere lake
The enchanting rough and tumble
Chained Cumbrian hills...

Like a worried teacher
Anxious that the fleeting pupil
Fully absorb what he, left alone
Must one day on his own remember
Drawn out of the depths of a retentive heart
That wasn't deaf and blind
When it wandered this path, admiring nature
With such peculiar urgency does this curve in the road
Where the road and the lake separate
And the woods begin, stand
Before my inner eye
Like an evening star long after the Sun has died…
A trigger, for when I focus
On that turn of the road, I see again
The rest of the walk
That followed it
Continues to follow me.

A familiar friend
    A giving, undemanding lover
A memory already more precious
Than Silver and Gold.

THE PRESENCE AMONGST THE LAKES

Incredible
You cannot be a poet amongst these hills
And not feel poetry come to you

Poems hang invisible above hills
Misty fruit, heavy, press upon the poet
Crave birth and eternity
The spoken and penned word
Cumbria
Heart of the Lake District

Waterfalls and mountain streams
Run into lakes
Constantly replenishing a poet's mind
Thousand thoughts and thousand dreams
Formed ethereally by poets forever unborn
Yet unthought, yet undreamed
Constantly regathering themselves
Atop

Misty hills
Waiting for the open and unsuspecting poet
Innocently passing by
Deep in thought
Musing over intuitions he thinks
Are his, deeply felt

Heavenly fishermen patiently await
A deep-diving spirit unafraid to emerge anew
New thoughts wander, as though by chance
Into the landscape of a poet's natural mind
There to be fructified and, once written down,
Passed on and eternalized.

There is a presence amongst these Lakes
Old as time
   Gentle as falling rain
      Forceful as a waterfall
         Calm as a Lake.

The poet's friend, Eternal Hills
Sleeping still, waking still.

THE SPIRIT THAT AWAKENED IN THE WOODS, HILLS AND LAKES

What has been the point of all that toil?
City's prisoner, corporate spoil
A long line of sleeping, not being alive
Continuous weeping
Waiting for the day I'll be reaping
That, after which I strive.

My heart has been leaping, trying to see the sun
Beeping, calling for the sun
Until my heart was full to the point of bursting
Full of longing
Blossoming of a full sense of belonging
Deep has been my thirsting –

This holiday, like a holy stay, in Gras- and Windermere
What have you done to me? Suddenly so clear
The poet in me again, ready to go his way
To be confronted
By all the effects of a life he's always wanted
Work is as play.

There is no alternative to being who you should be
No wealth, comfort, security will make you happy truly
Nothing can compensate a spirit for a wasted life
A deep sense of guilt
At death, crumbling, the empty life that was built
Has not soothed the inner strife.

Boldly go your way, seek no reward, Bravery
Must be your natural part, unaffected, unwavering –
No poet ever wrote for money who served Inspiration
The path is the goal
The burning of the Spirit Flame deep within the Soul
Unpoisoned by Ovation.

LAKE SPIRIT

My heart weeps, a baby
Another mountain stream
Seeking a lake
After which it longs, a Lover
Longing for completion
During the course of a life-long journey
Into the eternal sea.

My heart cries for that presence
That was his quiet audience
On a walk across a Valley
In a Cumbrian mystery –

Spirit, I know you can move
Through time and space. Find me, do,
Meet me, be with me, deeply,
No matter where I wander
Or rest my head at night – stay close, meander
Like a melody in my Soul...

I've run out of control
Searching for my Goal.

Cumbrian Lines

AN OBSERVANT LAKE

How much of it is left?
How much of the mist
Still revisits my mornings
Before my thoughts come calling?

From afar, I
Mean from gazing
Across time, it
Is a wonder to hold in
Your heart a
Thing that never
Fades, never
Weakens, changes
Never, teaches you how

To know the
Things you really
Love. They are the
Ones you never
Forget.

This carry with you as you mature
Measure with this everything you nurture
The camera behind your mind
Will click and capture
A lifelong picture
Of the things that slipped through,
The people and places that got to the core of you.

It will continue to happen inside, an observant lake
Like another part of you.

2.

INTUITIONS

BEHIND YOUR MIND

Insight awakens
What hope is there for Sight?
No matter what your eyes see outwardly
Your heart insists on knowing better inwardly
Proof is intellectual
Knowledge perceptual
A Dream will insist
Reality is the dreamy Mist.

Vision takes over
You become a tool of its mission
Lose your power of decision
In matters beyond the mind
There the mind is blind –
Your Vision does for you the Seeing
Makes of you a true human being
The mind sees the light
Bows to the inner power of Insight.

You search for words to speak your mind
Your strange heart is all you'll find.

CLEAR SIGHT

What is this haze?
My mind becomes a maze
My feet remember their ways
By memory always –

The things we learned by heart
The surest chart
In our last days

Adult becomes child anew
See what the child once saw in morning Dew.

STRONG AND STRONGER

How much longer
Must I keep growing stronger
Stronger everyday - ?

What yesterday I pushed away
Returns today, stronger
With even more hunger
Songs that I must play.

I have to move
Fly like a dove
Driven by love

I have to remove
Myself from illusion
Confusion.

Unfinished Verses stare at me
Repeated Verses endlessly.

Cumbrian Lines

EVENING

A dreamer sits by a lake
Reflecting, watching images
Dance upon still waters
Cover his mind

Hoping in the images
A mirror of his future
An Understanding of his path
To find –

The thousand eyes of the mind
Before the heart's gaze are blind.
Yet heart and mind are entwined
From the moment of birth
Into this earth.

Another day draws to a close
Another thorn, another rose
Have bled his toes
Healed his sorrows.

I want to hold him, tell him
To stop gazing upon his thoughts –
But he alone knows
These ways he follows.

REMEMBERING A POET FAR AWAY...

Remembering a friend far away
Whose thoughts come here every day
Whose spirit drew deep of the Inspiration
From poets of a distant nation
For we poets all from an invisible Kingdom come
United by intuitive wisdom.

His spirit walks with me unseen
Deeply felt he has always been
His words recall themselves to me
At many a detail gazing I see.
My Cumbrian holiday is his Victory indeed
For he sowed the precious seed.

Birthed far and wide ever
Yet switched on and off by the same lever
Simple Vision afflicts every true poet
We recognize the path, but how many go it?
Few in number, but we shall not slumber
On and on we quietly wander...

for Taiwo Onesi Dominic

Cumbrian Lines

SUNNY PATCHES

Sometimes the Sun came through
Through you
Sometimes the Sun shone through
I saw you
Constant by my side like the Sun
I turn and turn, but you are never gone.

Sometimes the Sun showed through
Through every hill
Sometimes the Sun waved through
I stood still
Until my heart, like a camera
Had taken in all it wished to one day remember.

Special sun, sparingly applied
By nature upon this fragile countryside
Delicacy, snapshots of Perfection
Stoking slowly Rising affection
Ray after ray, between misty showers
A Lover's advances after hours...
Stoking slowly Rising Affection
Countryside bathed in heaven's attention
Delicacy, snapshots of Perfection –
Contemplation, Redemption.
Those moments were ours.

Sometimes the Sun shone through
Through you, dear, through you
It was over before it started
New thoughts through my mind darted.
A flower smiled, waved Hello
Hello you too, happy Fellow...

POETRY IN EVERYTHING

She stands by the roadside
Smoking her thoughts away
Thoughts she tried
Could not find the words to say
Arise dejectedly, smoke and ashes
The green light flashes.

One last drag, last sigh
Last attempt to inwardly see the way
Shoulders sag, the look in her eye
When she turns briefly her head our way
Before stepping off across the road
Is itself a long and winding road.

A Cumbrian mountain-walk
Winding past trees and waterfalls
Feet heavied, it's your heart bears the bulk
Of any stray Sorrow that calls
Many strange paths will cross your feet
Follow not every path you meet...

A short smile crosses her face
Our eyes meet, a moment of connection
A smile at once everything unitable in one place
Joy, sorrow, interest, disaffection
The smile's source is its end
Just made and lost a friend.

Deep, the heart of every wanderer
Your path is the outgrowth of your heart
Gently touch, gently leave each sojourner
Take solely what the moment did impart
There'll bo onough in it to sorrow or sing
Poetry lurks in everything.

A moment in time, no content, no words
A mighty happening just played itself out
She crosses the road, I turn off at the boards
Never again will our paths cross, no doubt –
My woman walking beside me the whole time
Did she sense at all this passing rhyme?

The small, silent things that come and go
Without our really paying attention
The rock-solid things our hearts know
Even when we pay no attention –
The inner bond that withstands passing things
Takes note of the closing of little rings.

THOUGHTS WE MET

I won't forget
Every thought I met
Blowing in the breeze
Resting beneath the trees
Mirrored on each lake
Asleep or awake
Before which we waited
Silently contemplated
Another wonderful day
Of this lovely holiday…

Thoughts that grow
Flowers in the meadow
Time after time
Recurrent rhyme
Will yield new fruit
Magic flute
Even as I age
Page after page
Will always light the light
Of Insight.

3.

TO LEAVE IS TO STAY

FINAL MORNING IN THE
LAKE DISTRICT

Season of dream-like awakening
Morning of child-like perceiving
Awakening, dreaming, giving, Receiving
Consciousness of dawn breaking –
And overtaking; and leaving…

A holiday of deep perceiving indeed it has been
Even as we drove through these winding roads
In the heart of the lake district; it has been
As though these hills, these lakes, these woods, these
roads
Drove too through our heart and blood
Made themselves into a part of our Inner Abode
Where we have always been.

And life waited until you came into mine
Before it brought me here, you by my side
You who are my Inside Outside and my Outside Inside
In the presence of none other can I show such Intu-
itions fine
Like I've done by each Cumbrian lakeside
Grasmere or Windermere, Thirl or Ullswater
You have been to me like their gift, their daughter
Completed my heart quietly
Guided me tenderly
Been with me like the other me
Honestly, loyally.

Nothing much more to say –
The holiday, today, passes away
Leaves in its wake that which it has awakened
New life inside, never again to be forsaken
A poet, born again amongst these mists
Amidst these thoughts, a heart that forever persists...

If morning dawns on another day
You turn, find me not, I be faraway
Yet remember this morning which begins today
It heralds a Dawn that has come to stay –

Return we shall, my Dear
The Immovable rock each time the mists clear...
The poet's mind when acquired thoughts disappear –
Politicians gone, normal men and women
Speak the natural talk, show the natural acumen
Of the natural human. Walk that walk –
The walk is the immortalization of the talk.

A walk on the Cumbrian countryside
A gentle ride with human hearts open wide
Hearts that have smiled and mused, hearts that have
cried –
Hearts that have fused and have never died

THE LAST DAY IN A PLACE THAT REMINDS YOU OF PARADISE

The last day was the best
We paused to rest
Took in everything a second time
Knowing it would be the last time
For none can tell tomorrow –
Those that lend and those that borrow,
All are at the mercy of the Unexpected,
Certainty rests in the Unsuspected.
So we loved that Moment before it was past
Knowing it to be the last – Disappearing fast…

The last rain
The last mist
Again and again
Our hearts insist
Keep walking
Keep drinking
Stop talking
Stop thinking –
It's your future you're remembering here
Even before your spirits get there.
Wonder not how many lives you've lived in the mist,
Ask how much longer your spirits will exist –

Time to leave for the airport
We drive off, each the other's support
As we search now for what to do
With these new feelings, deep and true.

ONE LAST WAVE

This softness one more time
One final goodbye
Encompasses within me
A place I rarely reach
For it lies too deep for daily thoughts
But when it arises to the fore
Changes reality into folklore
That for one moment seems to last forevermore –

The Door. It is open.
The Spirit. It is woken.
The poem has come to its end –
Goodbye, my friend.

ON LEAVING THE LAKE DISTRICT

Not Goodbye will I say – Welcome
I feel Growing Blossom
Happening inside me

Curve has been squarely rounded
Crown has come unbounded
The past has untied me

Life, roller-coaster, upping, downing
Smiling, frowning; slaving, crowning
Villaging, towning; seriousing, clowning –
Take a gentle walk…

Gently into the Valley, gently up the Mountain
The MOMENT is the Reason, the Point, the Fountain,
Disappearing Chalk.

TIME STANDS STILL

Only a few days after
Already, that magical laughter
A wall-painting, hanging in time
There, at the back of my mind

I turn around with thoughtful eyes:

Time stands still; 'tis the spirit that flies.

MEMORY

It's already the Past

The Distant past
The Faraway past

Another era
Caught imperfectly on camera

Once upon a time...

AWAKENING AFTER A DREAM

Awakening out of a deeper reality
A dream of music, philosophy, poetry
Still ringing on in me, but fading fast
Each new second retaining less than the last
The dream fades away like an improbable past –
A populous sea into which a porous net is cast
The intellect tries to find again words, details
From each finishing dream but maddeningly fails –
Words which I just wrote down, somewhere, somehow
In a dream I was having sometime just right now
Melodies I was humming, natural realities I saw
I feel them still in me, but see them no more
For the heavy cloak and mind of a small and rigid earth
Have imprisoned again my consciousness, like once at
birth –

For as swiftly and surely as we once forgot the baby
thongue
As we grew from baby to child, yet remained young
So do words, connections given to us in our dreams
Oft disappear during Awakening, magically it seems
The harder the Intellect tries to affect their remember-
ing
The faster it hastens their forgetting –
Even while we are still lying, freshly awake, in the
morning bed
Watching one thing fading, another taking over, inside
our head
As one sun rises, another sun is setting gently –
The glass is unclear, twilight illuminates faintly
Dawn and Dusk together were breaking...
Wish I could remember who I really am, upon awaken-
ing.
Not acceptable, this unending sleep
Of an eternal consciousness in the Deep.

MORE AWARE OF NATURAL SOUNDS

The night is dark
African night
Wild with calls
Of insomniac frogs

A piercing screech
A thousand crickets
Cringe as one –

I drive and drive
Talking to my thoughts
Let them read
My inmost blogs

Should Death surprise
My drive tonight
It's good, I'm done –

My steps mount the stairs
The drive I did survive
Another day and night in the city
I'm still alive…

As I write down this poem
My neighbour's Airconditioning unit
Sounds like a Cumbrian waterfall rushing through my
heart –
It fills my ears
With the constant sound of the lonely beat of my heart.

EPILOGUE

Well, this place did strange things to me.

One, it gave me the perception of reincarnation. Made me feel like a wandering spirit that has lived in many strange places in many distant times, and this was one of them from some mysterious improbable past.

Two, it brought poetry back to me. Before visiting the Lake District with my then fiancée back in August of 2008, I had stopped writing poetry for a while and lost all interest in doing so. In the lake district it awakened again within me.

Three, I was finally able to visit the birth- and workplace of my all-time favourite poet William Wordsworth.

Four, it brought me close to nature and to spirit, to a sensing of eternity, of faraway and of inner voice.

Five, it deepened and cemented our love for each other.

What more could I ask for?

Che Chidi Chukwumerije

—

Cumbrian Lines
Poems born of the Lake District
August 2008

—

www.ingramcontent.com/pod-product-compliance
Lightning Source LLC
Chambersburg PA
CBHW020521030426
42337CB00011B/493